Knitting Beaded Purses
A Complete Guide to Creating Your Own

A How-to for Beginners

Schiffer Publishing Ltd®

4880 Lower Valley Road, Atglen, Pennsyl

Ncy VanDerPuy

ACKNOWLEDGEMENTS

I am grateful to my mom and dad, Ray and Evelyn Seven, who always encouraged me, and to my family of guys who could never understand my fascination with beads, but tolerated it anyway.

Thanks to the Sheboygan Bead Society and the knitting group at the Bahr Creek Llama Farm for showing interest in my passion.

I thank "A Vintage Shop" in Plymouth, Wisconsin for graciously lending me vintage clothing for photographs. To my models — Jodi Dulmes, Ruth VanDerPuy and Jessica Palm, a big thanks! I am also thankful for my son Tom's patient photography work.

To vintage purse collectors, Paula Higgins, Gay Wynveen, Madeline Hofer, Jodi Dulmes and others who wish to remain anonymous, I thank them for permission to use photographs of purses in their collections. Thanks to Kathy Burch of the Tri-State Antique Center for the use of purse pictures. Special thanks goes out to Lynell Schwartz, of The Curiosity Shop in Cheshire, Connecticut, for her advice and the use of some of the pictures from her books.

My highest praise goes to God for giving me the desire and the place to use my abilities. Luke 12:33, "Provide purses for yourselves that will not wear out, a treasure in heaven that will not be destroyed."

DEDICATION

To my three sisters, Phyl, Peggy and Barb — my best friends.

Other Schiffer Books on Related Subjects
Beading Necklaces, 0-88740-735-8, $12.95
How to Make Wonderful Porcelain Beads and Jewelry, 0-7643-2377-6, $19.95

Copyright © 2008 by Nancy VanDerPuy
Library of Congress Control Number: 2007940475

Designed by Martha Tyzenhouse
Type set in New Baskerville BT

ISBN: 978-0-7643-2870-1
Printed in China

Schiffer Books are available at special discounts for bulk purchases for sales promotions or premiums. Special editions, including personalized covers, corporate imprints, and excerpts can be created in large quantities for special needs. For more information contact the publisher:

Published by Schiffer Publishing Ltd.
4880 Lower Valley Road
Atglen, PA 19310
Phone: (610) 593-1777; Fax: (610) 593-2002
E-mail: Info@schifferbooks.com

For the largest selection of fine reference books on this and related subjects, please visit our web site at
www.schifferbooks.com
We are always looking for people to write books on new and related subjects. If you have an idea for a book please contact us at the above address.

This book may be purchased from the publisher.
Include $3.95 for shipping.
Please try your bookstore first.
You may write for a free catalog.

In Europe, Schiffer books are distributed by
Bushwood Books

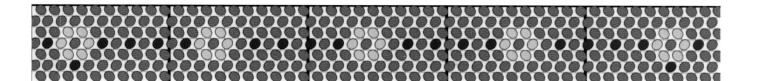

CONTENTS

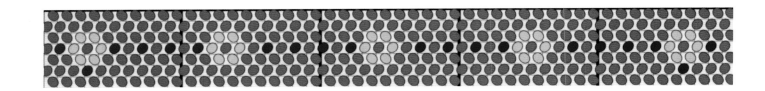

INTRODUCTION

When my mom made me go to our local yarn store in Wheaton, Illinois, forty years ago, I was ambivalent about taking knitting lessons. Yes, I learned to knit, but just barely. I put the half-finished lime green turtleneck in the back of my closet — where it sat for several years. I just wasn't motivated. Yarn stores' choices were basic — worsted weight, sport weight and fingering. The colors were equally uninspired.

Fast forward to the 1970s: I was in college where knitting and crocheting was becoming trendy; we all made lacy vests, ponchos, and plant hangers. I even finished that turtleneck. For most people, it was just a trend, but not for me. I started knitting with everything in sight — macramé cord, ribbon, and string. I made clothes, home décor, and even a bikini. And no one was safe from my gifts. I knitted dolls, hot pads, mittens, Christmas ornaments, pillows, Afghans, and every kind of sweater.

On to 1998: I continued to knit every kind of item imaginable, but I had yet to discover what would become my passion. I lived in Sheboygan, Wisconsin with my husband and two sons. The kids were in high school, and since I was a stay-at-home mom, I had a little time on my hands. I volunteered at the Sheboy-gan County Historical Museum for several years. In the museum's collection were some antique beaded purses, which another employee and I admired. Jodi Dulmes was a bead worker and became interested in the history of these purses. Coming across some antique purse instruction books, she shared them with me. I was never the same again.

I learned from the instruction books that most of the beaded purses of the eighteenth and nineteenth centuries were knit. The more I studied them, the more I said, "I can do that." But it was easier said than done. The books told what materials to use and even showed charts, but the beads and thread, were, of course, obsolete. They didn't tell me how to actually get the beads on the stitches!

I did a lot of experimentation and research, which was of very little help to me. I could eventually produce some knitted beadwork, but it wasn't of quality. The beads slipped around on the stitches, I couldn't find good thread, and I didn't know much about beads. Enter two particularly helpful resources.

While surfing for bead knitting web sites, I came across a video produced by Victorian Video Productions called, "Bead Knitting." Expert bead-knitter,

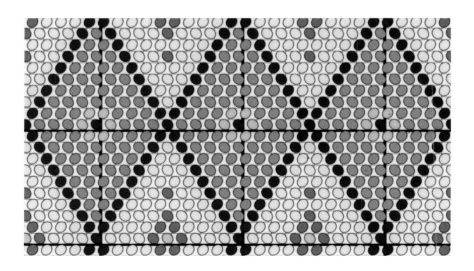

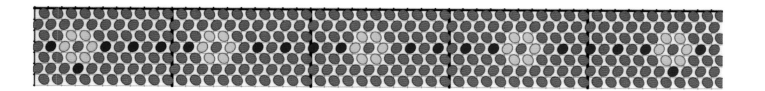

Alice Korach, showed how she produced beautiful, quality purses. This helped me tremendously to enhance my own technique based on some of the techniques she had developed. The other source that is a cornerstone for my skills is a book called *Mary Thomas's Knitting Book*, by Mary Thomas. It is an older book, but deftly describes not only basic knitting instructions, but also special techniques for bead knitting.

As helpful as these were, I still needed to develop my own way of bead knitting. I do basic knitting the "old" way, sometimes called "English," (or "British" or "American"), i.e. I carry the yarn in my right hand and throw the yarn over the right needle (as opposed to "Continental" knitting, where the yarn is carried in the left hand). I find this easiest, but maybe I'm just an "old dog." So I had to adapt some of the skills I learned from Ms. Korach and Ms. Thomas to my own habits.

I have also developed a unique charting system for making patterns. When I started bead knitting, there were very few patterns available. Patterns from other media (counted cross-stitch, bead weaving,

etc.) are usable, but turn out slightly skewed because the beads in bead knitting don't lay straight up and down, but diagonal. My charts are easy to follow and show exactly how the beads will lay on a completed project.

All of the patterns in this book draw their inspiration from antique beaded purses. I have included pictures of some of the purses that have moved me the most. But there are so many more that are beautiful examples of the talent of our Victorian sisters. Antique bead-knitted purses or pictures of them can be found on-line, in antique stores, in private collections, at estate sales, in museums and in books. They are in various stages of preservation, but they all inspire awe.

This book assumes you have some knitting experience. If you don't, use the lessons in Chapter Three to practice. There are also many good on-line instructional videos for basic knitting that you may find helpful: *www.knittinghelp.com* and *www.diynetwork.com*, or *www.hgtv.com*. For those of you who know how to knit and would like to learn how to enhance your work with beads, read on!

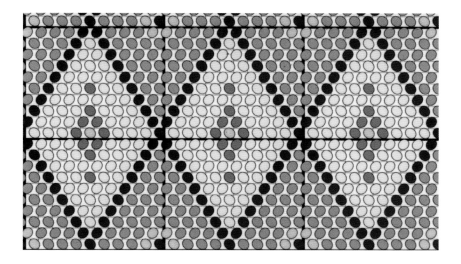

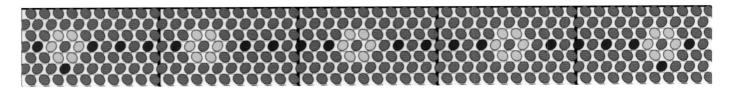

Chapter One:

WHAT IS BEAD KNITTING?

There is Beaded Knitting, and then there is Bead Knitting. The two crafts are similar in that both are used to put beads on knitted work. Below is a chart that helps differentiate the two methods.

CHARACTERISTIC	BEADED KNITTING	BEAD KNITTING
Difficulty	Easiest	Hardest
Bead Placement	Between stitches	On the stitches
# of Bead Colors	One	Many
Knit Stitches Used	Knit	Knit & Purl
Time	Less	More
Stringing Beads	From a hank	One by one, per chart
Key Advantage	Heavy, nice feel	Detailed look

A detailed discussion of Bead Knitting versus Beaded Knitting can be found on www.baglady.com.

Here are some pictures of Beaded Knit Items:

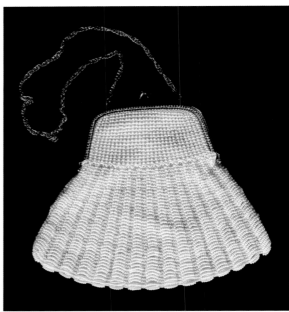

A beaded knit Purse

A beaded knit Amulet Bag

A beaded knit Amulet Bag

A fancy beaded knit purse made by the author. The design is by Barbara Pratt. *Courtesy of Jodi Dulmes.*

Bead Knitting is the more difficult of the two crafts. I prefer it because it allows for the use of many colors and in fact, pictorial knitting. Many antique and Victorian beaded purses featured pictures of castles, people and flowers. This is only possible in Bead Knitting because each bead is placed on a specific stitch, according to a chart, and the beads, whether knit from the front (knit stitch) or from the back (purl stitch), show only on the right side of the work.

Besides purses, bead knitting can be used for sweaters and scarves (as an embellishment), pillows, and many home décor items, but as far as I'm concerned, the highest and best use is for beaded purses!

An antique beaded purse with a parrot design from the author's collection.

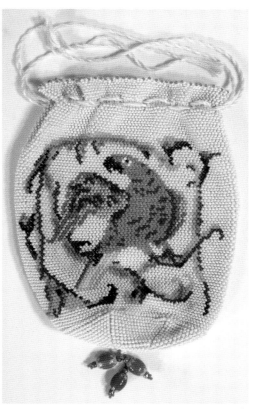

Author Nancy VanDerPuy created this piece using the motif of the Antique Parrot Purse.

Alisoun, in Chaucer's, *A Miller's Tale.*

Though beads have been in use for over 40,000 years, "little beaded bags" are a relatively modern phenomenon. Beaded purses for use as women's accessories started showing up in Europe several hundred years ago. Earliest purses were drawstring bags, called "reticules." Later, artisans attached their beadwork to frames, from very simple metal frames to elaborate jeweled or enameled frames.

Art and literature of the fourteenth and fifteenth centuries indicated that beaded purses were already in use at that time. Geoffrey Chaucer, in *The Miller's Tale* from *Canterbury Tales*, writes, "From her girdle hung a leathern purse tasseled with silk and with beads of latten."[1]

Some of the earliest beaded purses were created by skilled artisans, using silk thread and fine glass beads, as small as size thirty. One type of early beadwork was called Sablé (grain of sand) and originated in Paris. The beads were so tiny that a needle wouldn't go through the holes. The fine silk thread either had to be stiffened to go through the bead or be drawn through with a human hair.[2]

Patterns were created and fiercely guarded and the resulting purses were singular works of art. To carry one of these fine beaded purses was an indication of wealth and status. At this time, pictorial beadwork was popular, particularly castle purses. Highly skilled artisans also liked to use the motifs of famous paintings for their purse patterns. Most of the pictorial purses were bead-knit.

In the nineteenth century, beadwork became a craft for women to do at home. This work still required great skill and a good eye, as the beads were still very tiny, patterns had to be created on a grid, and the beads had to be strung in order on the fine thread. As beaded bags continued to gain popularity, several companies saw the wisdom in mass-producing materials and patterns. By the mid-nineteenth century, creating bead-knitted bags was a popular hobby. Some of the patterns still exist and purses created from those patterns can be seen in collections. Beaded purses that have survived for years, sometimes over a hundred years, are highly prized by collectors. Bags that are in excellent condition can be worth thousands of dollars.

Antique geometric design purse. *Courtesy of Jodi Dulmes.*

Antique Flowered Purse. *Courtesy of Gay Wynveen.*

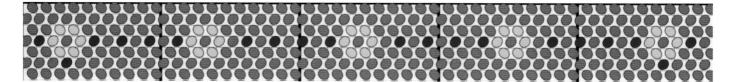

Chapter Two:

MATERIALS

Beads

Any material that could possibly be shaped into a bead has, at one time or another, been used to create a bead. Earliest beads, dating to thousands of years B.C., were crafted from animal teeth, bone, wood, ivory and seeds. Later, with the use of more technologically superior tools, beads were made from stone, gems, metals and glass. Beads have been made in every area of the world. In fact, beads are such a universal phenomenon that the study of beads has helped anthropologists learn about ancient cultures and how they interacted with each other. Beads are found in almost every ancient ruin in the world. I experienced one of the highlights of my "bead" life at Chaco Canyon in New Mexico. While exploring the extensive Puebloan dwellings dating back to the A.D. 850 - 1250, I happened to glance down at a large anthill. Among the dirt debris that formed the cone, I spotted tiny turquoise beads, brought up from deep below, by the industrious ants.

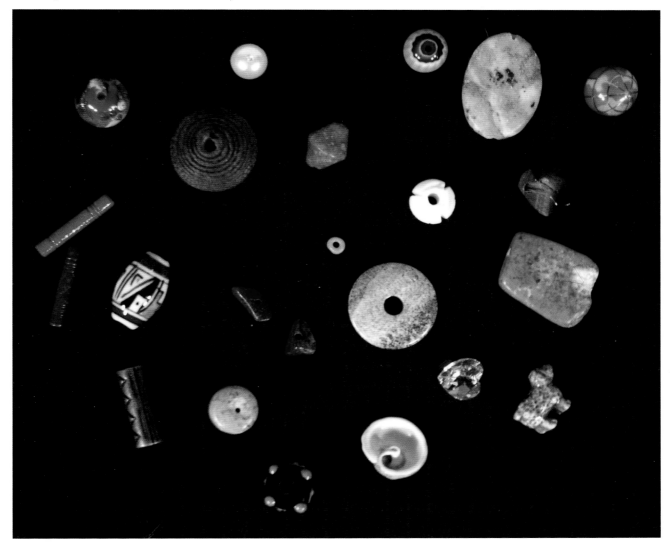

All types and colors of beads, ancient and modern

As varied as bead materials, so also are the uses for beads throughout the world and time. The North American Indians used them for trade and adornment, but long before that, they were used for anything from status symbols to religious ceremonies. Progression in the use of beads seemed to follow the level of industrialization of a culture; i.e. the more advanced a group was, the more their beads tended to be used for art and jewelry. It wasn't until about the fourteenth and fifteenth centuries, when glass beads started to be mass-produced, that beads became overwhelmingly used for adornment and ornament. It was at that time that Venice became a center for glass bead production. The Italian bead industry's secrets were as closely guarded as those of today's manufacturing giants, and this allowed Venice to remain the primary place for bead production for a long time. Since then, other areas of the world have come and gone as bead capitals, and today, Czechoslovakia and Japan hold that title.

All of the projects in this book are made with size 11 seed beads. This is the most common size bead and can be found in a variety of colors and finishes. Most bead stores carry Czech and Japanese seed beads. Czech beads are often strung on hanks (twelve strings of beads tied together), and Japanese beads generally come in plastic tubes.

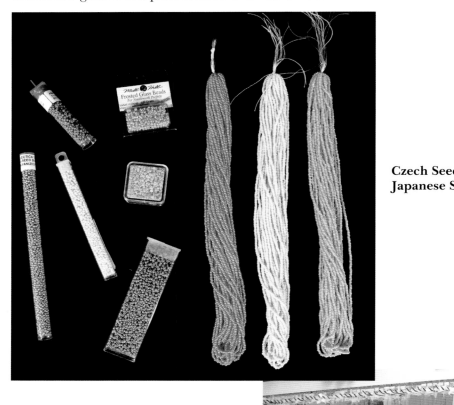

Czech Seed Beads (hank) and Japanese Seed Beads (tube)

Rows of Size 11 Czech Seed Bead hanks in a store.
Courtesy of Eclectica, Brookfield, Wisconsin.

Though quality, color, and finish vary among manufacturers, most Size 11 seed beads are interchangeable. All projects can also be done in size 8 seed beads (larger than 11s) or size 15 seed beads (smaller than 11s), but the size of the purse will be larger or smaller, respectively. Most antique purses were done with size 15 seed beads, or smaller, as in Sablé beadwork. This allows the picture to be very fine and detailed, but must have caused the knitter severe eye problems!

There is almost an unlimited choice of colors and finishes among size 11 seed beads and every bead worker has their favorites. Some are shiny, and some are dull. Projects can contain different types of beads; they can contain only one type for consistency. Below is a table of the most common seed bead finishes.

Bead Type	Characteristics
Transparent	Bead glass is transparent, usually shiny
Opaque	Solid color; somewhat shiny or dull
Rainbow/Iris	Finish has several colors or highlights
Pearl	Pearl-like look
Luster	Softly reflective, not shiny
Matte	Dull and smooth
Lined	Hole is lined with color
Ceylon	Pearl-like look
Metallic	Gold, Silver, Copper look

Seed beads also come with round or square holes, and can be faceted. For the projects in this book, I have used only round-hole, non-faceted beads.

I used size 11 seed beads for the main body of each purse. My fringe patterns are generally made of size 11 seed beads, but I've used some size 8 seed beads and some larger, decorative beads. Decorative or focal beads are so varied and beautiful that the choice is almost limitless. Any given bead store may not carry the same beads that I have used, but they will carry many bead choices that will be appropriate for your purses.

In the specific directions for each purse, I have given general seed bead colors. I do not list specific bead numbers for two reasons: one, numbers vary between manufacturer and country of origin; and two, you should feel free to use colors and types of seed beads that strike your fancy. For some of the patterns, I have created the same purse with slightly different beads so you can see how different types work together. Some of these purses are pictured at the end of Chapter Four.

Don't be afraid to mix bead types in your designs. The "Lucerne," as shown in Chapter Four, is a good example of mixed types. I like the look of shiny beads for water, but matte beads for the castle.

There is no right or wrong in choosing beads for bead knitting. Experiment with color and surface finish. Studying color and using a color wheel may enhance inspiration. Margie Deeb, in her book, *The Beader's Guide to Color*, says, "Extraordinary use of color emerges from both knowledge and a depth of personal expression."[3] Go to a bead store and gather colors together to see how they work together. Feel the flow of beads on hanks. Hold them up together so they mingle. You'll soon find you have favorite types and favorite color mixes. My personal favorite bead is a Hematite. It has a deeper sheen than almost any bead and seems to glow. Its color is hard to describe — it's black, blue, gray, and steel all combined into

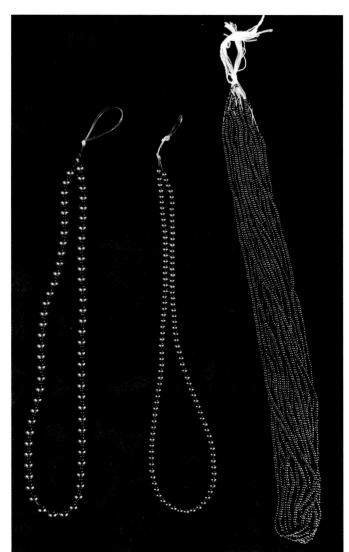

Hematite beads

Before buying beads, be sure to look them over carefully. There are many levels of quality even within the same color and finish; for example, an opaque ruby red seed bead from one manufacturer may be quite different from a product of another factory. A

one. The first purse, the "Madison," also described in Chapter Four, is made of Hematite seed beads.
A magnifying glass may help you determine if beads are of uniform shape and size.

Thread

For all of the projects in this book, I've used DMC Size 8 Perle Cotton. This is a good, basic thread. Other good cotton threads are Anchor Pearl Cotton Size 8 or Perle Finca No. 8 by Presencia Hilaturas S.A.

A more expensive, more durable, and supple thread is silk. A good brand is the Gudebrod Brothers Champion Silk size F. This is a good choice for a project that will be a keepsake for many years to come.

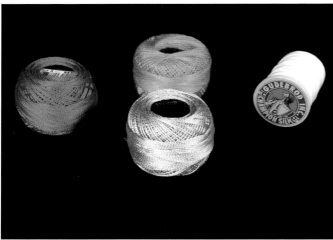

Samples of size 8 thread

Other Materials

The following supplies are available in any craft store. Most of these are necessary to complete the projects in this book, but some of them are marked with an asterisk (*), indicating that these are optional. In developing my own techniques, I have found these optional supplies are helpful, but you may find something else is more useful. *White foam pad, like "Funky Foam" or "Foamies:" I have found this is the best surface for threading beads. I use a 9" x 12" white sheet.

· Big Eye Needle (I prefer Darice "Easy Eye" Beading Needles #1144-26) for stringing beads onto thread
· Thread for stringing
· Miscellaneous decorative beads for embellishment
· Scrap paper for marking bead rows as they are threaded
· Small beading pliers for breaking misshapen or extra beads
· Small scissors
· Size 0000 Knitting Needles
· *Small corks for covering sharp points of knitting needles
· Cloths, like a washcloth, for winding strung beads, to keep them neat
· Bead Spinner (if stringing many beads of the same color that are purchased in tubes rather than hanks)
· *Fabric for lining
· Nymo Thread (Size D) for fringe
· Tapestry Needle (size 22) for sewing seams
· Beading Needle (size extra fine) for fringe
· Thread Heaven

A bead spinner

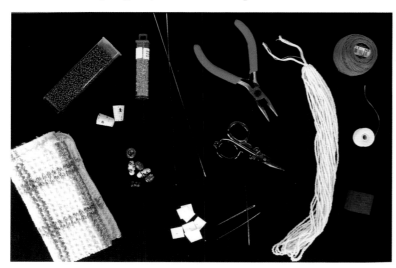

Materials used in bead knitting

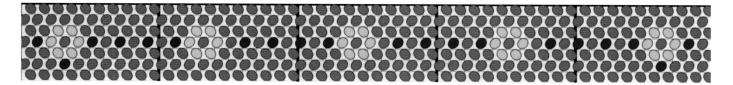

Chapter Three

TECHNIQUES

Basic Knitting

There are many different ways to achieve the basic knit stitch. The only thing they have in common is that the knitter uses two knitting needles and two hands! There are countless books and web sites that give basic knitting instruction. You'll have to find the technique that is easiest and most comfortable for you. The two most common knitting methods used in the United States today are the Continental and English methods. In the Continental way of knitting, the yarn is held in the left hand and guided easily around the needle tips. This method, if mastered, is a little faster. The English method is the most commonly used and taught method in the U.S. The yarn is held in the right hand and looped over the needles. Either method can be used for bead knitting. I am an English knitter and have been for forty years. I have tried the Continental method, but have always come back to the English!

There are also variations on the actual knit and purl stitch. Some knitters throw the yarn around the needle clockwise and some counter-clockwise. These techniques give the knitted fabric a slightly different look and are characteristic of knitting in different parts of the world, or used for a particular type of stitch. And then there are variations on which "leg" of the stitch is picked up.

If you're interested in bead knitting, you are probably already a knitter. But if you're not, I have included brief instructions for basic knitting. I begin with showing the English method for right-handed knitters. Then I will demonstrate other stitch basics for bead knitting.

If you are going to learn or practice basic knitting before attempting Bead Knitting, start with a pair of #8 needles and a ball of cotton worsted-weight yarn. In my instructions, I am using bamboo needles and Lily Sugar 'N Cream cotton yarn.

Casting On

There are several "Cast On" methods, but this is an easy one.

Leaving about an 18-inch tail, make a slip knot. Place the knot on your needle and tighten, but leave it loose enough to slide back and forth. Hold the tail to your left and the needle to your right.

A loop.

A loop through loop.

Pull the loop through loop to form a slip knot.

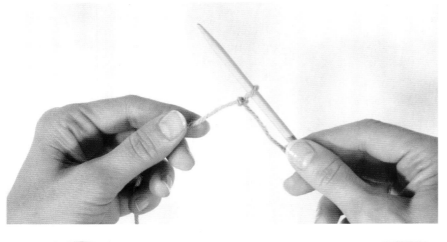

Put the slip knot on the needle.

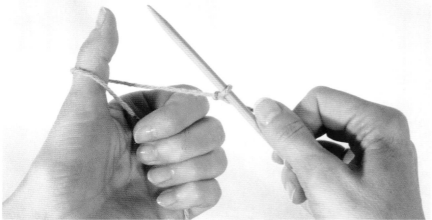

Around – Yarn in four fingers and around the thumb.

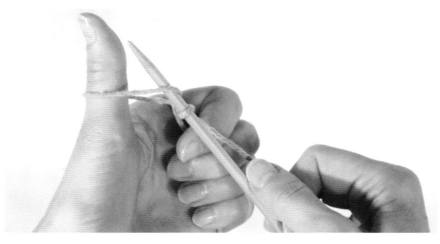

Through – Needle up through the loop on the thumb.

Circle – Right hand brings the yarn around the needle from the back.

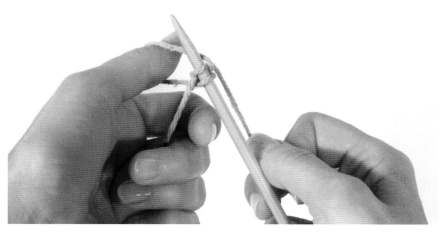

Over – Bring the loop on the left thumb over the needle.

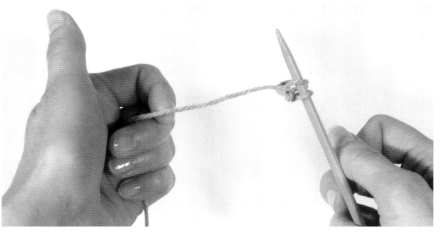

Snug – Pull the yarn snuggly, but not tightly to the needle.

Ten cast-on stitches

The Knit Stitch

Cast on as many stitches as you need to feel comfortable. When you are ready to proceed to the Knit Stitch, remove your practice cast on stitches and cast on twenty new stitches.

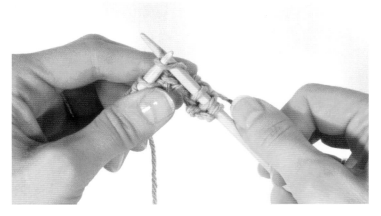

In – Needle goes through the front leg of the stitch, to the back of the work.

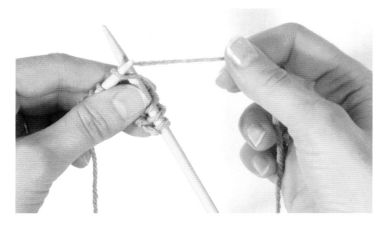

Around – Loop the yarn around the needle from the back to the front.

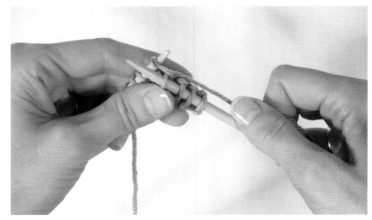

Under - Keeping tension on the yarn, pull the new loop under the stitch on the left needle.

Off – Pull the completed stitch off of the left needle.

Practice as many knit rows as needed to be comfortable with the knit stitch, then proceed to the next step — the Purl Stitch.

The Purl Stitch

For Bead Knitting the purses in this book, you will be knitting one row and purling one row. If you need practice with the purl stitch, practice the stitch as demonstrated below, on about twenty stitches.

In – Needle goes through front leg of the stitch, to the front of the work.

Under – Keeping tension on the yarn, pull the new loop under the stitch on the left needle

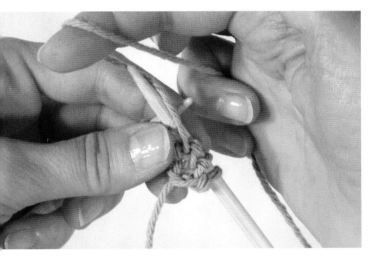

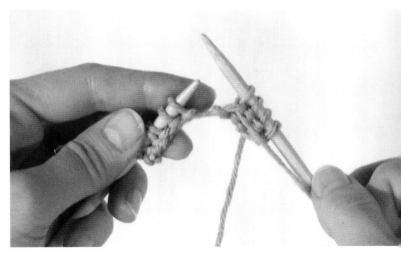

Around – Loop the yarn around the needle from back to front.

Off – Pull the completed stitch off of the left needle.

Binding Off

At the end of your finished piece, you'll need to "bind off" the stitches so it doesn't unravel. Again, there are many techniques for binding off — this is the most common.

Two – Knit or purl two stitches (depending on if you are working on a knit or purl row).

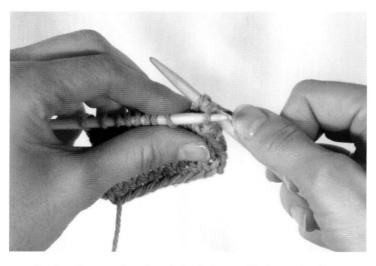

Grab – Insert the tip of the left needle into the first stitch (farthest to the right).

Draw – Draw the grabbed stitch over the other stitch and pull off of the right needle.

Again – Knit or purl another stitch and repeat grabbing and drawing.

Bound off the edge.

Yarn Over Stitch

This is one more stitch you'll need to learn to make the purses in this book. It is used to form the eyelets near the top of the purse for inserting the drawstring. A hole in the fabric is formed by knitting two stitches together and then bringing the yarn over the right needle.

A finished K2tog.

In – Needle goes through the front legs of two stitches together (abbreviation: K2tog, or K2, as in the patterns in this book).

Over – Bring the yarn around the right needle from back to front (abbreviation: YO).

Around – Loop the yarn around the needle from back to front.

Knit – Knit next stitch as usual.

An eyelet created by the K2YO.

A finished eyelet row showing two eyelets.

In the patterns in this book, this is done six times across the row. This stitch is indicated by "K2YO" on row seventy-one of all the patterns. The next row, a purl row, is done as usual, being careful to purl the yarn-over stitch as if it were a regular stitch. Then the purse is finished with seven more beaded rows and a cast off row.

Sewing Seams

The most common stitch to sew seams in knitting is the Mattress Stitch. Seams can be done in overcast stitch or several other methods, but the mattress stitch leaves an almost invisible seam. It takes a little practice, especially in bead knitting, because the stitches are so tiny, but the effort is worth it. Mattress Stitch is done with the two pieces of fabric right side up and laid along side of each other. Take the tail of one of the pieces and thread a tapestry needle. Join the other piece in the lower corner. Find the horizontal bar in each knit stitch as you go up the side of the fabric. Catch this bar on one piece of knitted fabric, then on the opposite piece, etc.

Catch the horizontal bar of the knit stitch on left-hand finished piece.

Mattress Stitch in progress.

You'll use the mattress stitch to sew up the sides and bottom of the purses. For the sides, use the same thread that you used for the purse, but for the bottom of the purse, use Nymo size D (which is used for fringe). When sewing up the bottom of the purse, you can use the mattress stitch, catching each cast on stitch instead of the horizontal bars.

Catch horizontal bar of the knit stitch immediately next to the bead on the left-hand finished piece.

Catch horizontal bar of the knit stitch immediately next to the bead on the right-hand finished piece.

Mattress Stitch in progress.

Practice Cast On, Knit, Purl and Bind Off on a small swatch. When you feel comfortable with it, introduce the stitch you will need to do Bead Knitting

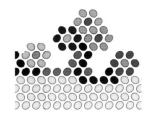

Bead Knitting Stitches

When beads are added to the knit fabric, they form a layer of beads on the right side of the knitting. The knit thread is almost unseen, behind the beads. If beads are added to regular knit stitches, they can "fall through" the stitches to the back of the fabric. Thus, the beads need to be "locked on" to the stitches. Giving each stitch a slight "twist" accomplishes this. Some experts have called this "Plaited Knitting."[4,5]

As mentioned before, a knit stitch can be achieved in a couple of different ways. The knitting tutorial above indicates that when doing a knit stitch, one inserts the right needle into the front "leg" of the stitch and brings the yarn counterclockwise around the right needle. In bead knitting, just the opposite is done.

In bead knitting, the right needle is inserted into the back "leg" of the stitch and the yarn is brought clockwise around the needle. Purl rows are done exactly the same as previously described, so the stitches are, in effect, twisted, making the knit fabric a little tighter. Holes between stitches are closed up a bit so the beads stay more firmly in the front of the fabric. Swatches show the difference between regular knit fabrics and "plaited" or "twisted" knit fabric.

Around – Loop the yarn around the needle from front to back.

A comparison of two knitting fabrics – Regular and Plaited.

In – Needle through the back leg of stitch, to the back of the work.

All patterns in this book are knit this way. The only time "regular" knitting is used is when knitting the eyelet row for the drawstring. Bead knit purses can also be knit in the round on four needles. In that case, rows alternate between one row of regular knitting and one row of twisted knitting.

Knitting with Beads

For practicing knitting with beads, I suggest using size 6 seed beads, a thin cotton or acrylic yarn (I used Red Heart Luster Sheen), and size 1 needles. You can use regular knitting needles or double-pointed needles. You'll also need a foam pad and a big-eye needle.

Lay a foam pad on the table and pour the beads onto the foam. Thread a big-eye needle with about ten yards of yarn (you can leave the thread attached to the skein). Thread about two hundred beads onto the thread. You'll want to move most of the beads on down the yarn for several feet. You'll use up the yarn faster than you'll use up the beads! Remove your threading needle.

Leaving a tail of about two feet, cast on twenty-four stitches, loosely. Purl one row loosely. In preparation for knitting the next row with beads, move about twenty beads up to within about four inches of your needles. Do the first two stitches, in twisted knit stitch (knit into back "leg" of stitch, yarn over needle clockwise) without beads for a selvage edge.

In – Needle through the back leg of the stitch, to the back of the work.

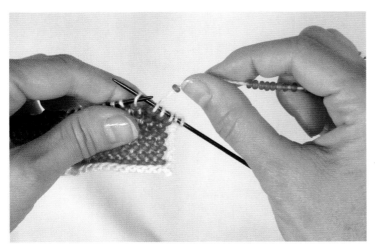

Up – Slide the bead up to within about a half inch of the needles.

Around – Loop the yarn around the needle from front to back, forcing the bead between the needles.

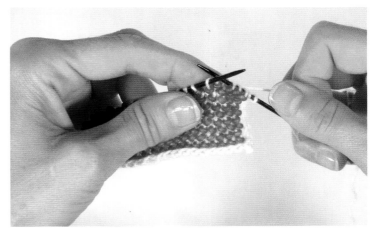

Through – With your left forefinger, pop the bead between the needles and to the front of the work.

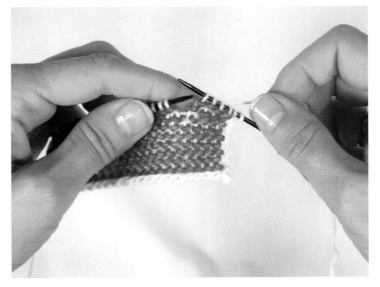

Off – Pull the completed stitch off of the left needle.

Knit with beads to last two stitches; knit last two stitches, also in twisted knit stitch. Purl next row with beads

23

The Purl Stitch

For the practice purl row, purl the first two stitches without beads, then purl twenty stitches with beads. Purl last two stitches without beads.

Continue knitting and purling until you have made a sample swatch of about twenty rows of bead knitting. If you'd like to try knitting with progressively smaller beads, try another swatch with size 8 beads, size 5-perle cotton and size 0 needles.

In – Put needle through the front leg of the stitch, to the front of the work.

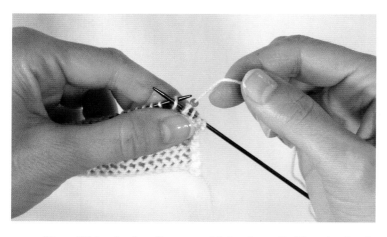

Up – Slide the bead up to within about half an inch of the needles.

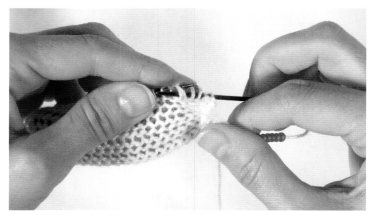

Around – Loop the yarn around the needle from back to front, forcing the bead between the needles.

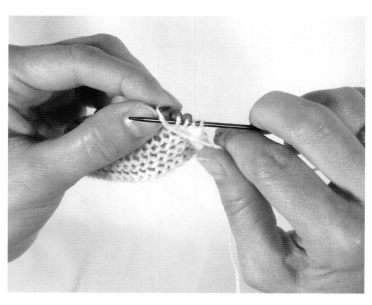

Through – With your left thumb, pop the bead between the needles and to the front of the work.

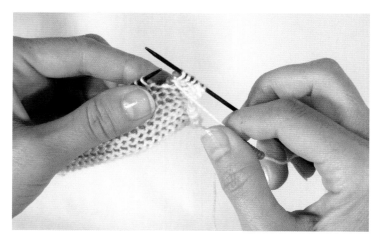

Off – Pull the completed stitch off of the left needle.

Below is a chart showing the appropriate size thread to use with several bead sizes. It's helpful in bead knitting to use a thread size that allows the beads to move easily, but not freely along the thread. In other words, the thread should be thick enough to hold the beads in place. When you are holding the beads close to the knitting needles, they should not be able to slide back down the thread, but should stay close to the needles.

Bead Size	Thread Size	Needle Size
6	Sport weight	1
8	#5 Perle Cotton	0
11	#8 Perle Cotton	0000
15	#12 Perle Cotton	000000

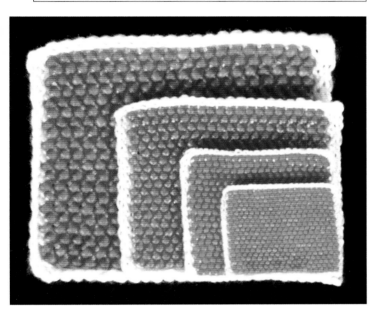

A comparison of bead knitting using different sized beads and thread.

Correcting Errors

From time to time you will make an error in stringing beads, you will drop a stitch, or a stitch will be misshapen. You'll want to go back and correct the error. There are several ways you can do this. If your error is only a row or two back, you can un-knit or un-purl up to the error. If the error is several rows back, you'll want to tear out the knitting to the point of the error.

Unknit Stitch — Slip the tip of the left needle into the stitch one row below, from behind.

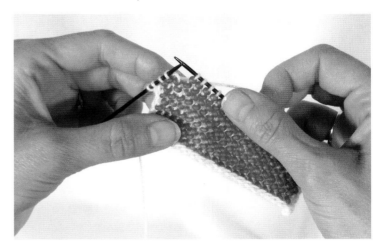

Slide the stitch off of the right needle and pull the stitch out with your right hand.

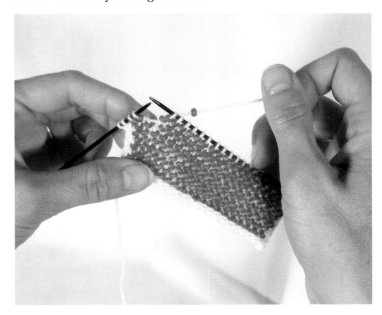

A completed Unknit Stitch.

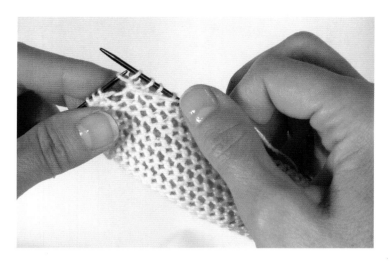

Unpurl Stitch – Slip the tip of the left needle into the stitch one row below, from behind.

If you have strung your beads incorrectly, you will have to cut the thread, correct the error, and re-string the beads. It's best to cut the thread at a side seam and re-string an entire row, rather than re-tying the thread in the middle of a row where a small hole might result.

You will usually catch your errors within a few stitches or rows, but if you don't, it's easy to tear out several rows of bead knitting. Insert a free needle into every stitch along a row, below your mistake. Remove working needle from last finished row. Carefully remove beaded stitches up to the free needle. Correct error and re-knit the removed rows.

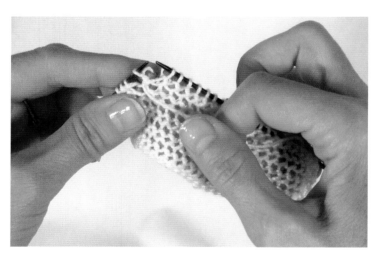

Slide the stitch off of the right needle and pull the stitch out with your right hand.

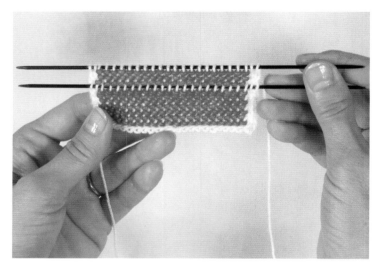

A free needle is inserted into each stitch of a row below the mistake.

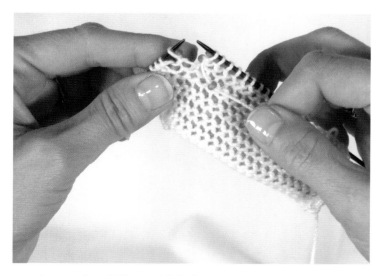

A completed Unpurl Stitch.

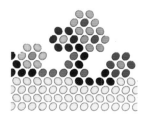

Reading a Pattern and Stringing Beads

The easiest purses to make are made of one color bead. No pattern grid is needed; the beads are strung on the knitting thread and knit, according to the number of beads per row and the number of rows. The simplest way to string these beads is to buy hanks of beads.

To begin knitting beads from a hank, you must slide the beads from the hank string onto your knitting thread. Simply tie one of the strands of beads from the hank onto your thread with a slipknot, pull the knot tight, but not locked, and slide the beads from the hank onto your thread.

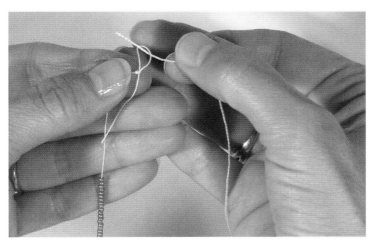

A knot for the sliding beads from the hank thread to the working thread.

If you are using only one color bead for a purse, you do not need to mark the rows with paper markers, but be careful to make sure you have fifty beads (as per the patterns in this book) in each completed row.

If a purse has more than one color, bead-knitting patterns are shone on a grid. They are similar to a counted cross stitch pattern grid, but because of the way the beads lie on the stitches, the rows are slightly tilted from each other, i.e. beads on knit rows point northwest and southeast; purl rows are just the opposite. Peyote Stitch and Brick Stitch patterns also offset the beads from each other, but the beads lie at a different orientation than in Bead Knitting. So patterns must be created specifically for bead knitting.

Beads are strung one at a time, one row at a time, starting at the last bead to be knit, and ending with the first bead to be knit. For the sample, you would first thread the beads in row twenty, starting at the arrow. Then you thread row nineteen, starting at the arrow, etc. The last bead you string in row one is the first bead you will knit.

Bead patterns show only the beaded stitches. Always add two stitches without beads to the beginning and end of each row.

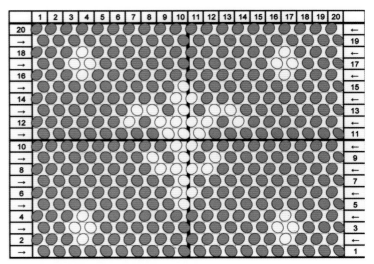

Sample chart of twenty rows.

Heavier lines on the chart mark every ten rows or ten beads. When stringing beads, it helps to count in each section of ten as you are stringing, "one, two, three..." up to ten. Doing so will help you keep your place in the pattern. For the sample and the patterns in this book, you will need the following materials:
· Foam Pad
   · Size 11 Seed Beads
   · Size 8 Cotton Perle
   · Big Eye Needle (I prefer the Darice "Easy Eye" Beading Needle #1144-26)
   · Scrap Paper cut into approx ½" x ½" squares
   · Wash cloth or similar size cloth
   · Ruler or other straight edge

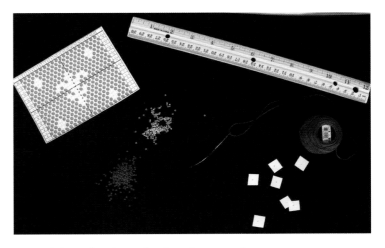

Materials to begin stringing the sampler.

Prepare the paper squares by laying them on the foam pad and puncturing each one in the middle with one of your knitting needles. Put them in a pile off to the side of your foam pad.

Paper row markers being punctured.

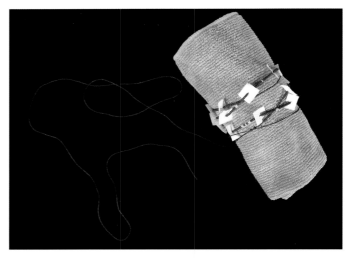

A beaded thread wound on a cloth.

Lay out the beads in color piles on the foam pad. Since I am right handed, I make the main color pile nearest my right hand. If there are some colors that are similar, separate them widely so they don't mingle. Thread the Big Eye Needle with the end of a Perle Cotton Ball; throw ball on floor and let about ten feet unwind. Lay the pattern as flat as possible above the foam pad. Lay a ruler or something with a straight edge on the pattern, above the first row you are going to string, as a guide.

Start stringing from the arrow on row twenty. After you string the first row, slide a paper marker onto the thread. Slide the beads and paper several feet down the thread. String the second row, slide on a paper marker, and so on. After stringing a number of rows, move some of the strung beads down the thread to the ball, stringing out the beads along ten to fifteen feet of thread. Trim off the first few feet of thread because it has been frayed from stringing, fold the cloth over the ball of thread, and roll the beaded thread around the cloth to keep it neat. Leave three to four feet of starting thread to cast on and purl the first row.

When making larger projects, like the purses in this book, you will need to string the purse in two parts, so as not to wear out the thread with too many beads being strung. For the purse patterns, string rows 40 – 1 and rows 79 – 41 separately. Knit rows 1 to 40, and then attach the second set of strung beads, and knit rows 41 through 79.

To make up a sample swatch from the pattern above cast on twenty-four stitches and purl one row.

On next row, working in "twisted" knitting, knit two stitches without beads, knit the twenty bead stitches, and knit two stitches without beads. Purl the next row by purling two stitches without beads, purl twenty bead stitches, and purl two stitches without beads. Continue on in this fashion until you finish the last beaded row. Bind off on the next row.

Shown is an idea for one thing you can do with your completed sampler.

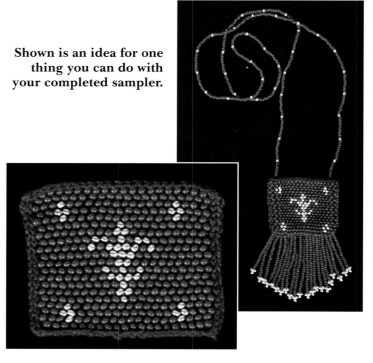

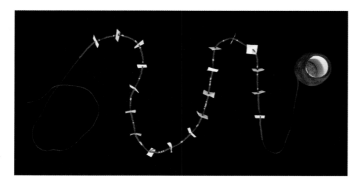

Shown is thread with beads strung and rows marked by paper markers.

A completed sampler.

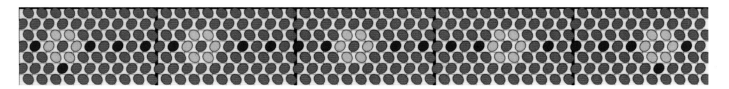

Chapter Four

PATTERNS

Basic Pattern Instructions

Below are instructions that are common to all of the patterns in this book. Anything that is special to a particular pattern will be listed in its instructions. All patterns are constructed in the same manner — a grid of fifty beads per row, seventy-nine rows altogether, and a three-row section that forms a drawstring casing. Gather the basic materials as discussed previously and begin to make the purse. String all the beads in two sections — Rows 79 to 41, and rows 40 to 1.

Cast on fifty-four stitches. Purl one row. On first row with beads, in "twisted" knitting, knit two stitches without beads, knit fifty bead stitches, and knit two stitches without beads. On next row, purl two stitches without beads, purl fifty bead stitches, and purl two stitches without beads. Continue in this way until the 69th row is completed. Purl one row without beads.

The next row is an eyelet row. This stitch pattern will form the holes for inserting the drawstring. This row is knit in REGULAR knitting (not twisted knitting, as for bead knitting), with no beads, with this pattern: knit six stitches, knit two stitches together,

and yarn over (K2YO). Continue like this to the end of the row, ending with six knit stitches.

The next row is purled without beads. Be sure to purl the "yarn over" stitches as if they were regular stitches. Finish this side of the purse with seven more rows of beads, and then cast off on the next row, which will be a purl row. Cast off as if you are purling.

Each purse measures about 4.5" x 6". Purse sizes can be easily changed by adding more or less beads to the rows or knitting more rows. Or, using larger beads will make a larger purse.

The second side of the purse is made exactly like the first side, with the exception of the "Antoinette." The backside of the "Antoinette" is strung so that the first and second sides flow into each other, with one continuous pattern.

Finish both sides of the purse, sew up the seams and decorate with fringe, if desired, by using one of the fringe options described in Chapter Five. Also, line, if desired, according to the directions in Chapter Five, or make a drawstring from ribbon, chain or silk cord. Finally, finish with a picot edging at the top, if desired, as per the instructions in Chapter Five.

The Patterns

The Madison

Introduction

This is a simple, elegant purse pattern. It can be embellished in a very simple or fancy way. Victorian women used plain beaded purses often. A plain black purse would have been the perfect accessory for a party or to use as a more every-day accompaniment. Nowadays, this simple purse, in any color, is a great gift for a bride or bridesmaid and can be decorated with an unlimited variety of fringes, decorative beads or ribbon drawstring.

This pattern is a simple bead knitting pattern in that it has only one color bead. Therefore, beads do not need to be strung in order. I have included a pattern and you may count out fifty beads per row if you desire. The beads can be strung a few different ways: by sliding the beads from a hank onto the knitting thread, by stringing the beads with a bead spinner, or by stringing the beads individually with a beading needle.

Materials

· 2-3 Hanks Hematite Size 11 Seed Beads
· 2 Balls black #8 Perle Cotton
· Miscellaneous decorative beads for fringe

From the collection of Paula Higgins; reprinted from Lynell Schwartz's *Vintage Purses at Their Best.*

From The Hiawatha Book.

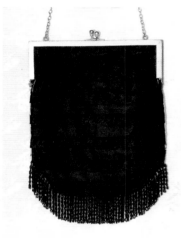

**The Madison —
The Author's Design.**

Chart for stringing beads for "The Madison."

The Rosemont

Introduction

This rose-patterned purse draws its design element from several samples of bead knitted purses of the eighteenth and nineteenth centuries. Flowers were a prominent design motif and appeared in many shapes, styles and colors. This pattern will give you an opportunity to learn to string several different colors of beads as you string the rose, but will allow you to string a simple pattern for the rest of the purse.

Materials

· Beads — Cream, Dark Rose, Medium Rose, Light Rose, Light Pink, Dark Green, Medium Green, Light Green
· Two Balls of Off White or Cream #8 Perle Cotton

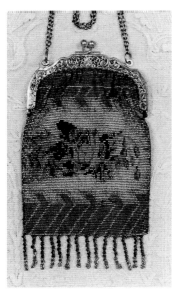

Reprinted from Lynell Schwartz's *Vintage Purses at Their Best.* **Photograph courtesy David Fowler.**

From the collection of Paula Higgins; reprinted from Lynell Schwartz's *Vintage Purses at Their Best.*

Reprinted from Lynell Schwartz's *Vintage Purses at Their Best. Photograph courtesy of David Fowler.*

Courtesy of tri-stateantiques.com.

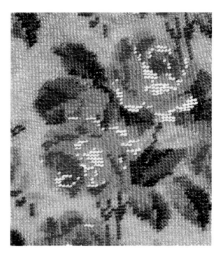

Close-up of beading. *Courtesy of tri-stateantiques.com.*

The Rosemont — The Author's Design.

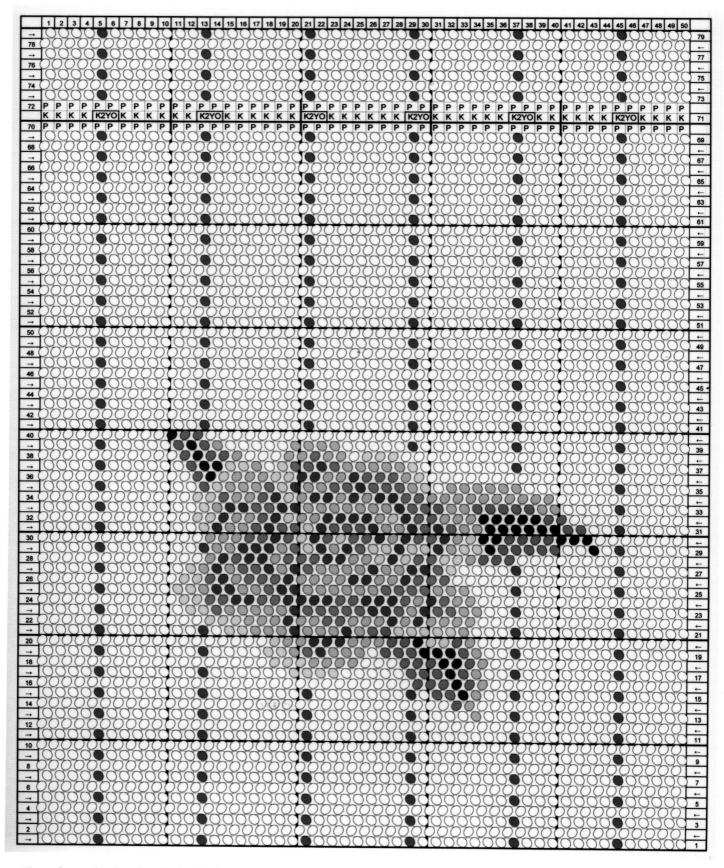

Chart for stringing beads for "The Rosemont."

34

The Highland

Introduction

The diagonal diamond pattern, or a variation of it, is found in a number of antique purses. What is appealing about it is the contrasting color. It is a good idea to bring out your color wheel in choosing your two main colors for this purse. Complimentary colors (on opposite sides of the color wheel) marry well in this purse, and the decorative colors could be colors that contrast with the two main color beads.

Materials

· Beads — Purple, Dark Purple, Light Yellow, Dark Yellow, Bright Green
· Two balls of Lavender #8 Perle Cotton

The Curiosity Shop. Reprinted from Lynell Schwartz's *Purse Masterpieces*.

Courtesy of tri-stateantiques.com.

From the collection of Paula Higgins; reprinted from Lynell Schwartz's *Purse Masterpieces*.

The Highland — The Author's Design.

Chart for stringing beads for "The Highland."

The Ashoka

Introduction

The "Carpet" motif is common in Victorian beaded purses. The theme is largely drawn from Persian designs, but other themes can also be found. American Indian influences can be seen in English and American beaded purses of later years; some Asian motifs are even found in some carpet design purses. The design is timeless and the geometric look is pleasing.

Materials

· Beads — Brick Red, Navy Blue, Green, Yellow
· Two balls of deep red #8 Perle Cotton

From the collection of Paula Higgins; reprinted from Lynell Schwartz's *Vintage Purses at Their Best.*

Courtesy of tri-stateantiques.com.

From the collection of Paula Higgins; reprinted from Lynell Schwartz's *Vintage Purses at Their Best.*

Courtesy of tri-stateantiques.com.

The Ashoka — The Author's Design.

Chart for stringing beads for "The Ashoka."

The Somerset

Introduction

There are so many floral-design purses from Victorian times that it is hard to choose which ones to feature. One of my favorite designs is a central floral design outlined by a contrasting color. The contrasting color is often black, but an off-white border makes a more airy, spring-like look. The bottom part of this pattern is difficult to string and requires concentration, but the top part is simply one color. You may wish to string rows 50 through 1 at one time, and then string the rest from hanks. You'll need about four hank strands to string the top part of this purse.

Materials
· Beads — Off-White or Cream, White, Dark Rose, Light Rose, Pink, Dark Orange, Light Orange, Yellow, Dark Green, Light Green, Dark Purple, Light Purple
· Two balls of Off-White or Cream #8 Perle Cotton

(Author's design, next page.)

From the collection of Paula Higgins; Reprinted from Lynell Schwartz's *Purse Masterpieces.*

The Curiosity Shop. Reprinted from Lynell Schwartz's *Purse Masterpieces.*

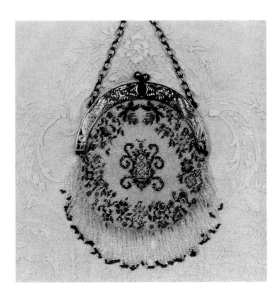

From the collection of Madeline Hofer; reprinted from Lynell Schwartz's *Vintage Purses at Their Best. Photograph courtesy of David Fowler.*

Reprinted from Lynell Schwartz's *Vintage Purses at Their Best. Photograph courtesy of Harry Barth.*

The Somerset — The Author's Design.

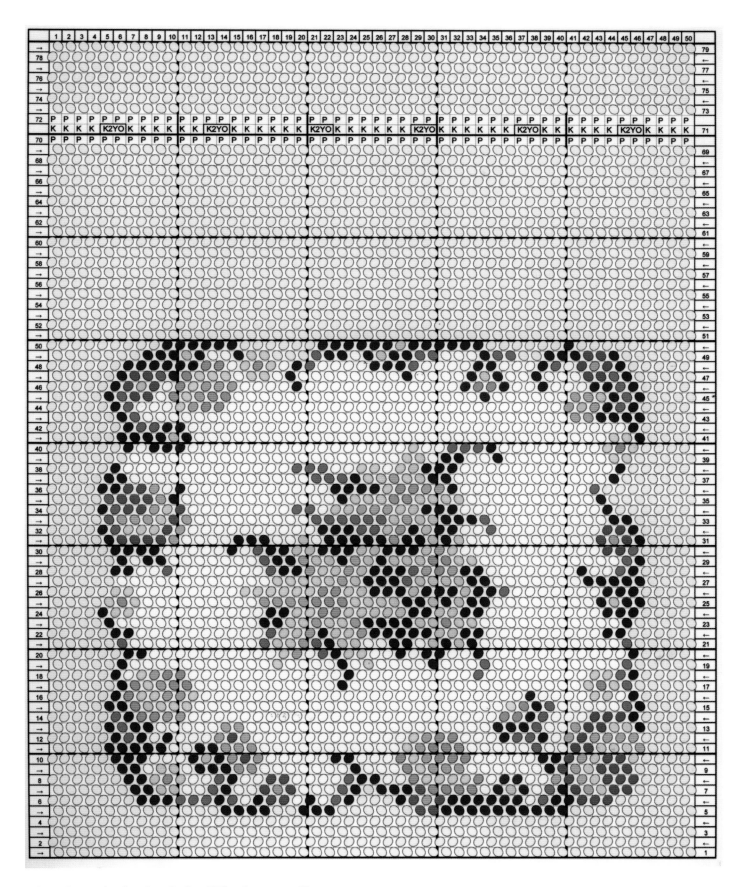

Chart for stringing beads for "The Somerset."

The Antoinette

Introduction

This purse is a little different in that there are two patterns — one for each side. The repeating pattern must be strung so that the finished purse will appear to have one continuous pattern from front to back. The side seams should be sewn carefully in mattress stitch so that the patterns come together smoothly.

The Fleur de Lis pattern has been a popular motif for centuries. It was frequently used in purses and other beaded accessories. Its use in this purse also recalls a pattern theme of a two-color repeat, which is frequently found in purses of the nineteenth century. I've re-created it in this Antoinette purse, and added a touch of red for interest.

Materials

· Beads — Matte Black, Metallic Silver, Bright Red
· Two balls Black #8 Perle Cotton

The New Bead Book. Reprinted from Lynell Schwartz's *Vintage Purses at Their Best.*

The Fleur-De-Lis
Model No. 787—A Crocheted Bag
Materials: 2 spools maroon purse twist; 10 bunches cut steel beads.

Chain 200 and join.

1st row: s.c. around.

3 rows of b.s.c.

2 rows s.c.

7th row: 10 b.s.c., 1 s.c.—around.

8th row: 1 b.s.c., 8 s.c., 1 b.s.c., 1 s.c., 1 b.s.c.—around.

9th row: 1 b.s.c., 1 s.c., 6 b.s.c., 1 s.c., 1 b.s.c., 1 s.c., 1 b.s.c.—around.

10th row: 1 b.s.c., 1 s.c., 1 b.s.c., 4 s.c., 1 b.s.c., 1 s.c., 1 b.s.c., 1 s.c., 1 b.s.c.—around.

11th row: 1 b.s.c., 1 s.c., 1 b.s.c., 1 s.c., 4 s.c., 1 s.c., 1 b.s.c., 1 s.c., 1 b.s.c.—around.

12th row: 1 b.s.c., 1 s.c., 1 b.s.c., 1 s.c., 1 b.s.c., 4 s.c., 1 b.s.c., 1 s.c., 1 b.s.c.—around.

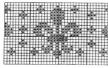

Diagram No. 3 — Unit of Fleur-de-lis.

Diagram No. 4 — Unit of border.

13th row: 1 b.s.c., 1 s.c., 1 b.s.c., 1 s.c., 6 b.s.c., 1 s.c., 1 b.s.c.—around.

14th row: 1 b.s.c., 1 s.c., 1 b.s.c., 8 s.c., 1 b.s.c.—around.

15th row: 1 b.s.c., 1 s.c., 10 b.s.c.—around.

2 rows of s.c.

3 rows of b.s.c.

2 rows of s.c.

23d row: 12 s.c., 1 b.s.c., 23 s.c., 1 b.s.c.—around.

24th row: 4 s.c., 1 b.s.c., 6 s.c., 3 b.s.c., 6 s.c., 1 b.s.c., 7 s.c., 1 b.s.c., 6 s.c., 3 b.s.c.—around.

25th row: 3 s.c., 3 b.s.c., 2 s.c., 2 b.s.c., 1 s.c., 3 b.s.c., 1 s.c., 2 b.s.c., 2 s.c., 3 b.s.c., 5 s.c., 3 b.s.c., 2 s.c.—around.

26th row: 4 s.c., 1 b.s.c., 2 s.c., 4 b.s.c., 1 s.c., 1 b.s.c., 1 s.c., 4 b.s.c., 2 s.c., 1 b.s.c., 7 s.c., 1 b.s.c., 2 s.c.—around.

27th row: 1 b.s.c., 6 s.c., 1 b.s.c., 1 s.c., 2 b.s.c., 1 s.c., 1 b.s.c., 1 s.c., 2 b.s.c., 1 s.c., 1 b.s.c., 6 s.c., 1 b.s.c., 6 s.c.—around.

28th row: 2 b.s.c., 8 s.c., 1 b.s.c., 1 s.c., 1 b.s.c., 1 s.c., 1 b.s.c., 8 s.c., 3 b.s.c., 8 s.c.—around.

29th row: 1 b.s.c., 8 s.c., 7 b.s.c., 8 s.c., 1 b.s.c., 8 s.c., 7 b.s.c.—around.

30th row: 9 s.c., 7 b.s.c., 17 s.c., 7 b.s.c.—around.

31st row: 5 s.c., 3 b.s.c., 2 s.c., 5 b.s.c., 3 b.s.c., 9 s.c., 3 b.s.c.—around.

32d row: 1 b.s.c., 3 s.c., 3 b.s.c., 2 s.c., 2 b.s.c., 1 s.c., 1 b.s.c., 1 s.c., 2 b.s.c., 2 s.c., 3 b.s.c., 3 s.c., 1 b.s.c., 3 s.c.—around.

33d row: 2 b.s.c., 2 s.c., 3 b.s.c., 1 s.c., 3 b.s.c., 1 s.c., 1 b.s.c., 1 s.c., 3 b.s.c., 1 s.c., 3 b.s.c., 2 s.c., 3 b.s.c., 2 s.c.—around.

34th row: 1 b.s.c., 4 s.c., 5 b.s.c., 2 s.c., 1 b.s.c., 2 s.c., 5 b.s.c., 4 s.c., 1 b.s.c., 4 s.c.—around.

35th row: 6 s.c., 3 b.s.c., 2 s.c., 3 b.s.c., 2 s.c., 3 b.s.c., 11 s.c.—around.

36th row: 11 s.c., 3 b.s.c., 21 s.c., 3 b.s.c.—around.

37th row: 1 b.s.c., 9 s.c., 5 b.s.c., 9 s.c., 1 b.s.c., 9 s.c., 5 b.s.c.—around.

38th row: 2 b.s.c., 8 s.c., 5 b.s.c., 8 s.c., 3 b.s.c., 8 s.c., 5 b.s.c.—around.

39th row: 1 b.s.c., 4 s.c., 1 b.s.c., 5 s.c., 5 b.s.c., 4 s.c., 1 b.s.c., 4 s.c., 1 b.s.c., 4 s.c.—around.

40th row: 4 s.c., 3 b.s.c., 4 s.c., 3 b.s.c., 4 s.c., 3 b.s.c., 7 s.c., 3 b.s.c., 4 s.c., 3 b.s.c.—around.

41st row: 5 s.c., 1 b.s.c., 6 s.c., 1 b.s.c., 6 s.c., 1 b.s.c., 9 s.c., 1 b.s.c., 6 s.c.—around.

42d row: 1 b.s.c., 23 s.c., 1 b.s.c., 23 s.c., 1 b.s.c.—around.

43d row: 2 b.s.c., 6 s.c., 1 b.s.c., 7 s.c., 1 b.s.c., 6 s.c., 3 b.s.c., 6 s.c., 1 b.s.c., 7 s.c., 1 b.s.c.—around.

44th row: 2 b.s.c., 1 s.c., 2 b.s.c., 2 s.c., 3 b.s.c., 5 s.c., 3 b.s.c., 2 s.c., 2 b.s.c., 1 s.c., 3 b.s.c., 1 s.c., 2 b.s.c.—around.

Follow fleur-de-lis pattern in same order as above.

Sew up bottom of bag and attach fringe.

If metal top is desired, sides can be left open at the top while crocheting, or slit down after the work is finished. Line the bag.

Reprinted from *Bead Work*, 2nd Edition. Courtesy of Lacis Publications.

Watch Fob with Fleur-de-Lis Pattern
Design No. 55 — Loom Work

Materials: Gold and black beads.

Cut 22 threads for loom. Fob is 21 beads wide.

String beads as per Diagram No. 12, decreasing at end for fastening over gold bar of fob clasp.

Diagram No. 12 of design No. 55.

Reprinted from *Bead Work*, 2nd Edition. Courtesy of Lacis Publications.

The BIARRITZ No. 600

Knitted Bag with Blue Silk Background. Spanish Butterfly and Bee Design in Steel Beads.

Made with HEMINWAY SILKS

Materials: No. 666 Navy, 2 spools Purse Twist, 9 bunches Steel Beads No. 8 or 9, ¼ yd. Silk or Satin for lining, 6 Brass Rings (½ inch diameter), 1 pair No. 18 Steel Knitting Needles.

Border at Top of Bag: String 3 bunches of Steel Beads (B.) on 1 spool of silk, cast on 89 sts. Knit (kn.) 3 rows plain. Throughout the design there is always a return row of plain knitting, this will not be mentioned again. As per diagram there is always 1 kn. st. on each side of bag. **4th row.**—Kn. 2 sts, * insert needle in next st., push a B. toward needle, kn. or complete the st., kn. 1, * repeat across row, end kn. 2 sts. **5th row.**—Kn. 1 st,

Concluded on page 7

89 stitches across – 106 ridges in length

Biarritz Bag No 600   Background in navy silk–design in steel beads

Reprinted from *Beaded Bags & More. Courtesy of Lacis Publications.*

No. 600

Reprinted from Beaded Bags & More. Courtesy of Lacis Publications.

The Antoinette — The Author's Design.

Chart for stringing beads for side one of "The Antoinette."

44

Chart for stringing beads for side two of "The Antoinette."

The Lucerne

Introduction

Of all the antique beaded purses, the Castle or Scenic purse is my favorite. Some of these purses are made with tiny beads no bigger than a grain of sand. Thus, the purse maker was able to show great detail. Many depict castles, houses, ships and even people in extraordinary likeness. Replicas of great works of art were often featured in scenic purses. I like to experiment with different types of beads for these scenic purses. Silver lined or rainbow finish beads work well for water; matte beads seem to display buildings with greater effect. But mountains, clouds, trees, and flowers can be drawn with various types of beads, with much different outcome. Have fun choosing beads for this purse.

Materials

· Beads — Light Blue (water and sky), Medium Blue (water), Dark Blue (water), Light Green, Medium Green, Dark Green, Lt. Purple, Dark Purple, Light Yellow (sand), White (clouds), Off White (castle), Beige (castle), Dark Brown (windows), Light Orange (roof), Dark Orange (roof)
· Two balls of White #8 Perle Cotton

Reprinted from Lynell Schwartz's *Purse Masterpieces.* **Photograph courtesy of Harry Barth.**

Reprinted from Lynell Schwartz's *Purse Masterpieces.*

Courtesy of tri-stateantiques.com.

The Lucerne — The Author's Design.

Chart for stringing beads for "The Lucerne."

Your purses can, of course, be made with different colors than are suggested in the patterns. Below are a few of the patterns created with different beads, different fringes and different drawstrings. The "Ashoka" has taken on a whole new look with the change of color and fringe, and should probably now be called the "Anasazi." The "Antoinette" has a lighter look with the new colors and addition of focal beads to the drawstring. The "Highland" now uses two beads of the same color, but in a matte and a sparkly version. It becomes much more sophisticated with the color change. The "Madison" in white would make a great bridal gift; the silver accents could just as easily be gold, and the flower shaped focal beads in the fringe give it a dressy look. The "Lucerne" hasn't changed much except for the fringe and a few minor colors and finish (shiny to matte) changes.Experiment with different seed bead colors, types and finishes. There are about as many combinations as you can imagine. I get a great deal of satisfaction just in the planning of a purse. In fact, when I come up with an idea, I often drop everything else on my schedule and go to the bead store. I hope you will feel the same passion to make beaded purses!

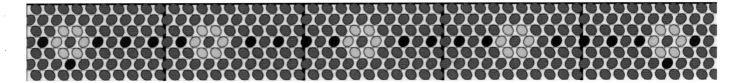

Chapter Five:

FINISHING

Since all the purses in this book are made from a basic pattern, construction of the purses will be fairly easy. The really creative part is adding your personal touch to each one. In this chapter, I demonstrate some ways that you can decorate your purse in a style you desire. Fringe is the most obvious accessory. There are limitless ways you can add fringe; I have described several, but you can adapt these in many ways. You can make fringe longer, shorter, thicker, more colorful, etc. You don't have to add fringe at all. You can even knit or crochet fringe. Experiment with different ways to add fringe.

I usually make a drawstring out of the same thread as the body of the purse, but there are many other things that can be used for a drawstring, such as ribbon, smooth chain, rickrack, etc. Use your imagination.

Lining your purse is optional. The knitted fabric makes a self-lining that is fairly sturdy, but you may want to line your purse for more durability. I have included a simple pattern and instructions.

And, you may want to dress up the top of your purse with a fancy, or "picot" edging.

FRINGE

Basic Fringe Instructions

Materials

Nymo Size D, Seed Beads to match purse, Miscellaneous Decorative Beads, Thread Heaven, Beading Needle

Shown are basic fringe materials.

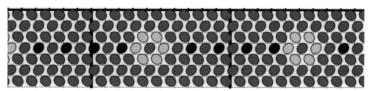

Basics

Cut a piece of Nymo about two yards long. Condition it with Thread Heaven by holding the thread down on the Thread Heaven box with a finger and drawing the thread across. Do this twice — once each way. Run the thread through your fingers to de-static the thread and straighten it.

From inside the purse, weave the Nymo into the right side seam of the purse, starting about 1.5 inches above the bottom seam. Weave for about one inch, knot, weave to the corner, and knot again. Bring the Nymo to the outside right corner and continue with fringe as per specific instructions.

It helps to knot Nymo after every three or four fringes to stabilize fringe and secure it.

Either side of purse can be the "right" side. Just determine which one you want it to be, and work from there. I find it easier to work fringe from right to left, but you may like to work left to right.

After completing the last fringe on the right corner of the purse, knot the thread and bring the needle and thread up into purse. Weave into seam for about a half-inch, knot, and weave about another half-inch. Cut thread.

Straight Fringe (The "Madison")

Bring the Nymo out of the purse at a bottom right corner. String thirty beads and push the beads up to the bottom of the purse. Skipping last bead strung (30th bead), bring the needle back up through twenty-nine beads, and bring the needle out at first bead strung, at the bottom of purse. Snug the beads up against bottom of purse.

Insert tip of needle back into the purse at the top of the fringe just completed, and back out again about 1/16th of an inch, or about one bead width, farther to the left of the fringe. Make another fringe. Continue across the bottom of purse.

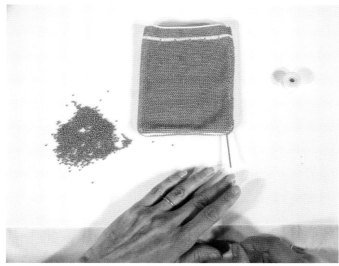

String thirty beads.

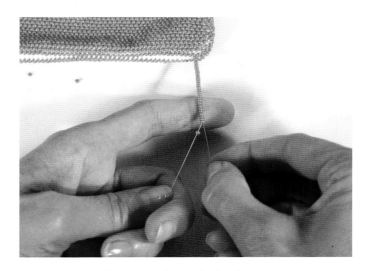

Thread Nymo back up through the fringe.

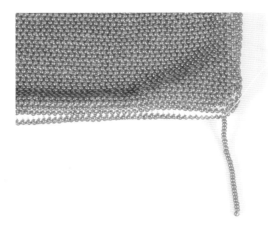

A completed fringe.

Make a decorative focal bead fringe (as on the "Madison"), after completing the straight fringe. Weave and knot the thread as before and bring it outside of the purse, about one inch from left seam. String thirty beads. String your choice of decorative or focal beads.

Skipping last seed bead (or beads), run thread back up along the decorative beads and seed beads, up through the first bead strung. Bring the needle back into the purse and pull up inside the purse, snugging the fringe tightly against bottom of purse.

Weave thread along the inside seams for about one inch to the middle of the bottom seam, and bring the thread to outside of the purse. Repeat beads for last fringe. Bring the thread into the purse, weave into the seam about one inch further, and bring to the outside to string the last of the three decorative fringes. Complete fringe and bring the thread to the inside of the purse. Weave in and knot as before, then cut thread.

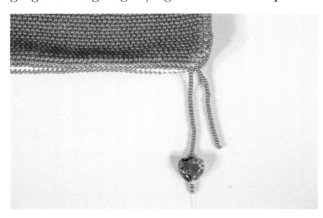

String thirty beads, focal bead, and more seed beads, if desired.

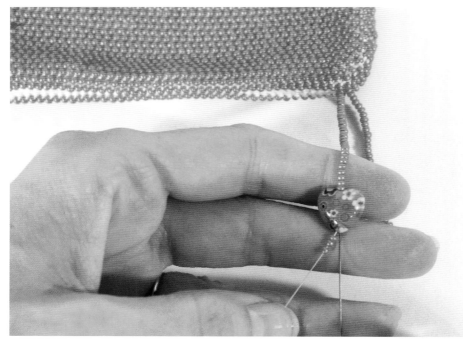

Thread Nymo back up through the fringe.

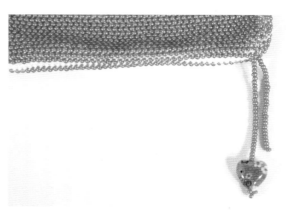

A finished fringe with decorative beads.

Interlocked Loops (The "Rosemont")

Follow the instructions for basic fringe, bringing the Nymo out of the purse at the bottom right corner of the purse. If making fringe of one color, string fifty to sixty beads; if using multiple colors (as on the "Rosemont"), thread twenty-five main color beads, three color A, three color B, three color A, and twenty-five main color.

First Fringe: Slide tightly up to the bottom of the purse. Insert the needle less than 1/4th of an inch from the first leg of the fringe and then come back out toward the first leg, about half way between the new insertion and the first leg.

Second and all following fringes: Thread beads as for first fringe. Bring the needle behind and through previous fringe. The two legs of the current fringe and the previous one will twist once. Continue on across bottom of the purse.

String another fifty to sixty beads.

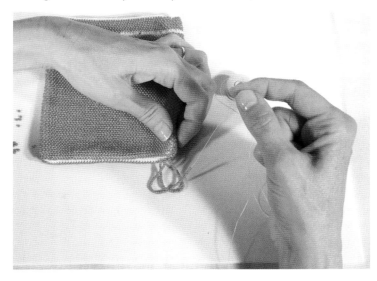

Bring the needle behind and through the previous fringe.

String fifty to sixty beads; use multiple colors if desired.

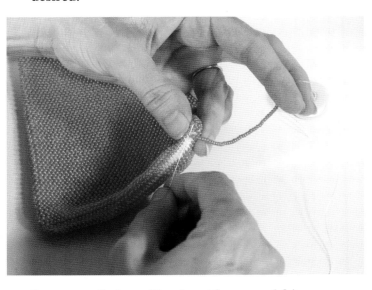

Insert needle in and back out for second fringe.

A finished Interlocking Loop Fringe.

Twisted Fringe (The "Ashoka")

Follow the instructions for basic fringe. Use beads to correspond with the main color of the purse. Use a Nymo similar to the color of Perle Cotton. Bring the Nymo thread to the outside lower right corner of the purse and thread fifty beads. Slide tightly up to bottom of the purse.

To make twist: Grasp thread just below the fifty beads with left thumb and forefinger tightly. With moistened right thumb and forefinger (Hint: If you're making this for yourself, you can lick your fingers here, but if it is for someone else, use a wet rag or fingertip moistener!), twist thread about seven times, each time securing the twist with your left thumb and forefinger. Thread will start twisting like a snake to the right of the beads. Push twists out to the length of the thread.

Thread must be allowed to untangle before you go further. With your left thumb and forefinger still grasping the thread tightly, use the other fingers of your left hand to hold up the purse high (you might stand up), let needle and loose thread dangle, and untangle. Make sure there are several inches of "tail" through the needle. This will help the needle stay on the thread as it dangles.

While still holding the thread in your left hand, stitch into the seam close to the current fringe. Come back out of the seam about 1/8th of an inch from the entry and make a knot to secure the thread.

You might want to hold the purse up and tidy up the new fringe. It should twist two to three times to the left. Use your fingers to manipulate it into a nice twist.

Start the next fringe by again threading about fifty beads. You should have about eight fringes per inch.

Grasp the thread.

Twist the thread.

A finished Twisted Fringe.

54

Looped Fringe (The "Lucerne")

Begin fringe as instructed in the Basic Fringe directions. If making this fringe from a one-color bead, string about forty beads. If making this fringe for a multi-colored purse, like the "Lucerne," use the three blue (water) colored beads and white Nymo. Position the thread to come out at the base of the first bead on the front corner. The fringe will start at the front side of the purse and end at the back of the purse. Thus, when you hold up the purse, you'll see the front side of the fringe; turn the purse around and you'll see the back side of the fringe. You will thread forty beads for each fringe. Each fringe will start on the front of the purse, string forty beads, insert the needle from the back of the purse (at the bottom row of knit beads), and bring back to the front of the purse, about bead length from previous fringe.

If making fringe on the "Lucerne," your purse will have light colored "water" to the right and darker "water" on the left. The back of the purse will be just the opposite. You will be threading beads in random patterns to mimic the watercolors. Make the loops so that beads will roughly correspond to the colors of beads at the bottom of the purse, on the side facing you. For example, when you thread the first half of the beads for each fringe, you'll try to match the front of the purse. The last half of the threaded beads will match the back of the purse. So, for the first fringe, thread about twenty light colored beads (interspersing a few dark beads for water effect). Then, to match the back of the purse, string twenty dark colored beads.

As you make fringes and progress to the left, gradually darken the mix of strung beads, so that by the middle of the purse, you are stringing mostly medium colored beads, then as you go further to the left, the first twenty beads are mostly dark and the last twenty beads are mostly light.

These fringe examples are just a few of the many fringe or decorative choices for finishing your purse. The "Somerset" uses only a few decorative beads for finishing. Some beaded purses look better with no fringe at all. Many of the antique beaded purses used fringe sparingly, or used a netted fringe. Use your imagination!

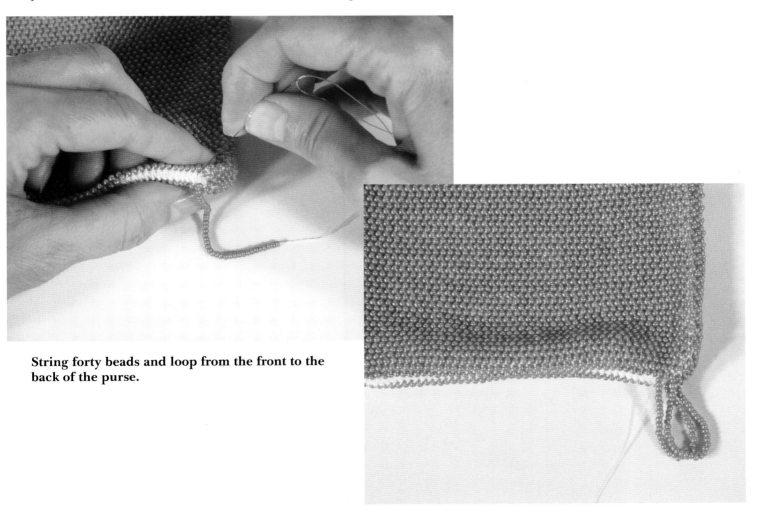

String forty beads and loop from the front to the back of the purse.

A finished Looped Fringe.

PICOT EDGING

A decorative edging on the top of the purse is optional. It gives the purse a bit more elegance and can be done with a one-color bead or it can pick up several colors from the purse beads.

Materials you will need are seed beads, a beading needle and Nymo thread. Thread the needle with about two inches of thread. Weave the thread through a side seam about one inch below the top of the purse, knot, and bring up the thread outside the purse just below last row of beads and near the seam. Bring the needle up through the first bead, string three beads, and bring needle down through next bead in row. A Picot of three beads is formed. Bring the needle up through the next bead in row, string three beads, and bring the needle down through the next bead. Continue around the top of the purse, back to the beginning point. Knot the thread into the fabric and weave loose end down into seam for about an inch.

Thread Nymo up through a bead.

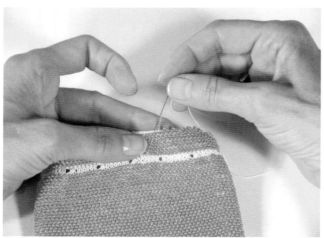

Thread Nymo down through the next bead.

A finished Picot.

THE DRAWSTRING

The drawstring for these purses can be made out of anything you can imagine, but a drawstring that is made out of the same material as the purse — Perle Cotton, is easy, durable and coordinates well with the purse.

Cut four strands of thread, each ten feet long. Fold two strands in half and tape the two cut ends together to a table. Place your index finger through looped end, and twist whole strand about 150 times until it gets tight on your finger. Fold strands in half by bringing the looped end up to the taped cut ends; at the same time, pull the center downward. Allow the strand to twist on by itself. This makes a drawstring about 2 ½ feet long. Make two.

Tie a tight knot in each end of the drawstring. This will facilitate threading it through the eyelet holes in the purse.

Begin threading from right side of the purse by bringing the drawstring from the outside to the inside through the first hole. Come back out in the next hole to the left, and so on, through all twelve holes in the purse. Thread second drawstring, starting from the opposite side.

Pull both drawstrings gently until the purse closes evenly. Measure about eight inches from the purse up one side of drawstring. Make a neat knot. Holding the purse up by the drawstrings, measure where to make a matching knot on the opposite drawstring. Trim about an inch up from the knot to finish.

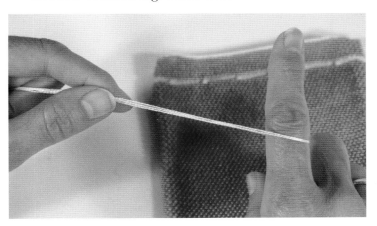

With your finger through the loop, twist the thread.

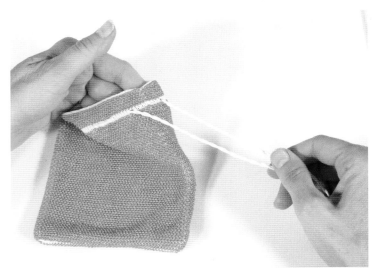

A threaded drawstring.

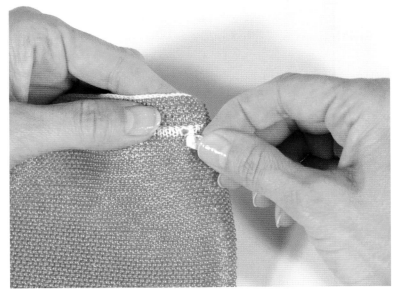

Thread the knot of the drawstring through the eyelets.

A finished drawstring.

Lining

A purse lining is optional. The inside knit fabric of your purse acts as a lining, of sorts, and this is sometimes sufficient. However, a lining can make your purse more durable, elegant and useful. With simple sewing skills, you can easily make a lining.

Choose a coordinating fabric for your lining. It can be as fancy as satin or as simple as cotton. One advantage of cotton or acrylic fabrics is their washability. But the big advantage of a silk or satin lining is its beauty and feel. The gift of a beaded purse is made even more special if it has a satin lining.

A finished lining.

Cut out two pieces of fabric according to the heavy lines of the pattern and sew on the dotted lines. Reinforce by going over the corners or an entire seam line and then trim the seams to about 1/4" to 1/8" of an inch. With wrong side out, fold top down half an inch. Insert lining into the purse, and line up the top of the lining with the knitted row just below the eyelet row of the purse. Pin in place and sew lining to purse.

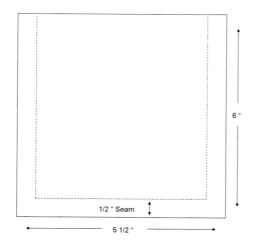

6 "

1/2 " Seam

5 1/2 "

Lining pattern

CARING FOR YOUR PURSE

Generally, the bead knitted purses in this book can be gently hand-washed and laid flat to dry. However, a few beads are not colorfast when put in water. Test some of each bead you are using for color-fastness by putting them in water overnight. If you line a purse with fabric, make sure it is washable before washing the purse. Some beads are also light sensitive. I have had beautiful white beads turn an ugly gray, in just a few hours, in direct sunlight.

If you are making a purse for display, it's best to show it lying down on a shelf or table, rather than hanging by its drawstring. Hanging is acceptable for a short time, but be aware that the purse will stretch out slightly over time.

When I start to design a new pattern, I generally start with a blank pattern and lightly sketch out my idea on the grid. Then I start to fill in the "beads" with colored pencil. This turns into a rough draft that I then copy to a new, clean grid, using colored pencils or pens.

For designing your own, I have provided the following sample blank pattern. This page may be photocopied for personal use if you would like to try to create your own pattern. It may not be copied for commercial use or for re-sale.

	1	2	3	4	5	6	7	8	9	10	11	12	13	14	15	16	17	18	19	20	21	22	23	24	25	26	27	28	29	30	31	32	33	34	35	36	37	38	39	40	41	42	43	44	45	46	47	48	49	50	

→ 78 / 79
→ 76 / 77 ←
→ 74 / 75
72 → / 73 ←

Row 72: P P P P P P P P P P P P P P P P P P P P P P P P P P P P P P P P P P P P P P P P P P P P P P P P P P

Row 71: K K K K K2YO K K K K K K K2YO K K K K K K K2YO K K K K K K K2YO K K K K K K K2YO K K K K K K K2YO K K K — 71

Row 70: P P P P P P P P P P P P P P P P P P P P P P P P P P P P P P P P P P P P P P P P P P P P P P P P P P

→ 70 / 69
68 → / 67 ←
→ 66 / 65 ←
64 → / 63 ←
→ 62 / 61 ←
60 → / 59 ←
→ 58 / 57 ←
56 → / 55 ←
→ 54 / 53 ←
52 → / 51 ←
50 → / 49 ←
→ 48 / 47 ←
→ 46 / 45 ←
→ 44 / 43 ←
→ 42 / 41 ←
40 → / 39 ←
→ 38 / 37 ←
→ 36 / 35 ←
→ 34 / 33 ←
→ 32 / 31 ←
30 → / 29 ←
→ 28 / 27 ←
→ 26 / 25 ←
→ 24 / 23 ←
→ 22 / 21 ←
20 → / 19 ←
→ 18 / 17 ←
→ 16 / 15 ←
→ 14 / 13 ←
→ 12 / 11 ←
10 → / 9 ←
→ 8 / 7 ←
→ 6 / 5 ←
→ 4 / 3 ←
→ 2 / 1 →

Row 16/15 area: K K K K2YO K K K K K K K2YO K K K K K2YO K K K K K K K2YO K K K K K K K2YO K K K K K K K2YO K K K K

59

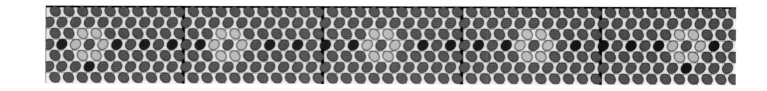

GALLERY

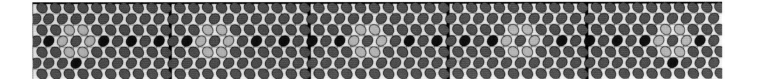

ENDNOTES

1   Tatlock, John S. P. and Percy MacKaye. *The Complete Poetical Works of Geoffrey Chaucer, Now First Put into Modern English*. New York, New York: Macmillan Company, 1912, 1940.

2   Higgins, Paula and Lori Blaser. *A Passion for Purses*. Atglen, Pennsylvania: Schiffer Publishing Ltd., 2007.

3   Deeb, Margie. *The Beader's Guide to Color*. New York, New York: Watson-Guptill Publications, a division of VNU Business Media, Inc., 2004.

4   Thomas, Mary. *Mary Thomas's Knitting Book*. New York, New York: Dover Publications, Inc. 1938. Reprinted 1972 by special arrangement with Hodder and Stoughton, Ltd., Warwick Lane, London, E.C.A.

5   "Bead Knitting." Video. Colfax, California: Victorian Video Productions, 1995.

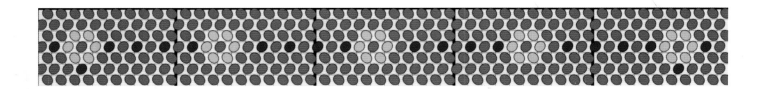

BIBLIOGRAPHY

Deeb, Margie. *The Beader's Guide to Color*. New York, New York: Watson-Guptill Publications, 2004.

Dubin, Lois Sherr. *The History of Beads*. New York, New York: Abradale Press, Harry N. Abrams, Inc., 1998.

Higgins, Paula, and Lori Blaser. *A Passion for Purses*. Atglen, Pennsylvania: Schiffer Publishing, Ltd., 2007.

Schwartz, Lynell K. *Purse Masterpieces*. Atglen, Pennsylvania: Schiffer Publishing, Ltd., 2004.

Schwartz, Lynell K. *Vintage Purses at Their Best*. Atglen, Pennsylvania: Schiffer Publishing, Ltd., 2004.

Tatlock, John S. P. and Percy MacKaye. *The Complete Poetical Works of Geoffrey Chaucer, Now First Put into Modern English*. New York, New York: Macmillan Company, 1912.

Thomas, Mary. *Mary Thomas's Knitting Book*. New York, New York: Dover Publications, Inc. 1938. Reprinted 1972 by special arrangement with Hodder and Stoughton, Ltd. Warwick Lane, London, E.C.A.

"Bead Knitting." Video. Colfax, California: Victorian Video Productions, 1995.

The Hiawatha Book. New York, New York: Dritz-Traum Co., 1924.

www.diynetwork.com

www.knittinghelp.com

www.hgtv.com

www.baglady.com

MATERIALS, SOURCES, SUPPLIERS

· Strukel Photography, Ltd., 3615 Erie Avenue, Sheboygan, Wisconsin 53081
· Eclectica, 18900 W. Bluemound Road, Brookfield, Wisconsin 53045
· JSM Bead Coop, 931 North 8th Street, Sheboygan, Wisconsin 53081
· Victorian Chocolate Shoppe, 519 S. 8th Street, Sheboygan, Wisconsin 53081
· A Vintage Shop, 227 E. Mill Street, Plymouth, Wisconsin 53073
· The Curiosity Shop, P. O. Box 964, Cheshire, Connecticut 06410
· Lacis Publications, 3163 Adeline Street, Berkeley, California 94703
· Herrschners, 2800 Hoover Road, Stevens Point, Wisconsin 54481
· Victorian Cottage Treasures, P. O. Box 752, Porthill, Idaho 83853
· Beadwrangler, 228 N. Sun Court, Tampa, Florida 33613
· BagLady, Inc., P. O. Box 2409, Evergreen, Colorado 80437
· Sheboygan County Historical Museum, 3110 Erie Avenue, Sheboygan, Wisconsin 53081
· Tri-State Antique Center, 47 W. Pike, Canonsburg, Pennsylvania 14317
· Barbara Pratt, Barb's Bags, www.barbsbags.com